SHE IS THE SUN

Collection of Poetry

Niccole Salm

SHE IS THE SUN

Copyright © 2021 by Niccole Salm. All rights reserved. Printed in the United States of America. No part of this book may be used or reproduced in any manner whatsoever without written permission except in the case of reprints in the context of reviews.

ISBN: 9798583113873

This collection of poetry is about power, resilience, overcoming hard times, and unleashing the chains we put on ourselves. These are stories of realizations, heartache, family trauma, healing, blooming love, and finding meaning. In my life I've learned that through the dark times, we must be our own source of light. We have to bring our own sunshine on a cloudy day. We must find ourselves and know our truth in order to learn our purpose.

- About the book

Written by

Niccole Salm

Edited by

Dianne Eltagunde

MY STORY

Never thought I'd have so many stories
Locked up inside of me
Bottled up emotions
Waiting to be set free

Stories of Heartache..................................11

Stories of Hope.....................................51

Stories of Love......................................89

Stories I Treasure the Most....................121

Everyone has their story
This is my tale to be told
So here is all of me

Being brave and being bold

Stories of Heartache
These are the times when we feel broken. This shattering feeling comes from family trauma, bad relationships, mental illness, and the weight of the world on our shoulders. When we experience overwhelming sadness, it can feel like we are isolated in our emotions. Although it can seem lonely at times, we all go through hardships. No matter how different we may be.

Stories of Hope
These are the moments where we feel like we're healing. We are evolving and discovering our purpose and who we are supposed to be. These are the stories that bring hopefulness to the future as we mend our broken hearts and tend to our battle scars. Healing is a process. It is a bumpy road along the way, but it's a mission we will accomplish.

Stories of Love
These are the stories that make our heart race. The moments in love where it gets intimate. The moments in love where it becomes serious, yet so simple. Those moments where we forget all the bad and the ugly in life. All because a love so beautiful swept you off your feet as if you've never been on the ground.

Stories I Treasure the Most
These are the stories of resilience. These are the moments when my soul feels like it's been set free. I am powering through the dark times and I am creating the light I always needed. These are the stories where I saved myself. These are the stories that will forever remind me that I am the one who gets to define who I am.

- The stories you will read

Stories of Heartache…

SHE IS THE SUN

My memory of you
Splattered like watercolor
Stroking my mind like a paintbrush

The blurry image of you and me
Watching artwork bleed on a canvas
Like a picture that takes me
Back to the past

- Watercolors

Niccole Salm

My eyes shed a tear before my eyelids even open
My heart reminds me I'm in pain
Before my brain can notice

The warmness of my blood
Takes over my whole body
All memories besides you
Become more and more foggy

Emotions come in waves
Crashing like the ocean
A wound that starts to heal
Just to be cut back open

I can't take my focus off the pain that takes over
Every day that passes I hope that I get closer

To mending my heart that's beat up black and blue
But how the hell do people expect
Me to get over you

- The aftermath

SHE IS THE SUN

I turn up my car speaker
To drown out my thoughts
But who knew
The louder the music gets
The more I think of you

    -   Don't want to think about you

Niccole Salm

Sometimes
I miss hearing the sound of your voice
Then I remember
How the words you spoke
Put my heart through the
Worst of dangers

- Proceed with caution

SHE IS THE SUN

You filled me with doubt
Buried me in wrongful shame
So deep
I thought I'd never escape

      - Let me out

You lost her

And maybe you wish
You could've done things differently
Maybe you would've loved her a little harder
And loved other women a little less

Loyalty is one of her best qualities
And now you're all alone
Because you can't say the same thing

That's what happens
When you steer your boat
Into the middle of the ocean
You threw out your compass and
Navigated with emotion
Because you wanted to see what else was out there

You lose her

- A lost love in deep water

Winter has no contest
On your ice cold heart
Who knew a gentle breeze and light snowfall
Could make me feel
So damn small

    -   Cold as you

Niccole Salm

He gets caught up in his ways
Cause that's just how he is
He's a game you're bound to lose
More like a stranger to the truth

He's a dangerous situation
Like a product of temptation
Someone you thought you could trust
Turns out his morals are unfair and unjust

I guess I was a fool for thinking
He could ever change
Inside I know there is a boy
Who was not born this way

Maybe it was stress
That led him on a path to drinking
Maybe there's a chance for change
Or maybe that's just wishful thinking

- Too late for change

He always rolled the dice
Cause he thought he was lucky
Thought he'd win the jackpot
Before all hell got ugly
Isn't it funny how the gambling man
Does everything and all he can
But when he played the odds

He played himself

- The house always wins

If you were half the man you claim to be
You wouldn't have settled for a girl
Who isn't even worth
Half of me

- Irreplaceable

SHE IS THE SUN

You guys can have one another
Because with hearts that ugly
You two deserve each other

- Don't forget what comes around goes around

Every day is a rehearsal
For the performer that lives in you
You don't need a stage
Or a fake character's name
Because acting like someone you're not
Isn't very new to you

Sounding like a broken record
Time and time again
Life giving you another chance
You keep taking it and then…

Out running your responsibilities
Till this day I don't know
How you got this far in life
Or even get away with it now

You put on a great show
With the mask you always wear
Round of applause for the performer
For the truth will not be spared

- Standing ovation

You have an ace up your sleeve
A wild card in your heart
The man at the poker table
Making gambling an art

You play your cards
And raise the bets
Without a reason or a plan
I guess that's why they call you

River man

- King of hearts

Niccole Salm

Do you think the sun and the moon
Reach out for each other
Trying to stretch across the sky
Constantly chasing each other around the earth
Only to be disappointed that they cannot be together
Because they serve the world better
When they are apart

- Like me and you

SHE IS THE SUN

The sun rises
As this side of the world
Starts a new day
The crisp morning air
Fills the atmosphere

As adults go to work
As children go to school

Busyness spreads across the awakening city
As my eyes open
As my mind begins to ponder
I can't help but wonder

Who is on your mind first thing in the morning
And are they laying right beside you

- Who is waking up in your arms

Niccole Salm

Would you seek me in a crowd
Would you listen for my voice in a sea of people
Or would you rather
Care not to bother
Because treating me like a stranger
Makes getting over me

That much easier

    -   Out of sight, out of mind

I convinced myself
That healing was a waste of time
Because it took more energy to heal
Than it did to hurt

- When it's easier to be sad

I hate how much I love you
But I hate me a little more
And I can't stand the fact that I don't remember
What I hate you for

- Love/hate relationships

SHE IS THE SUN

Only you can drive me this crazy
Drive me mad
Making me insane
I figured I'd just face it
Cause some things never change

Addicted to the chaos
Attracted to the mess
You'd think I know better
But I haven't learned just yet

- Don't know any better

Niccole Salm

If the world was ending
Would you cry out for me

Would you search for me
In your last moments
Or would you just

Let it be

    -   If the end was near

SHE IS THE SUN

I just wanted you in my corner

I've taken so many hits and dirty blows
In the ring defending you
I thought maybe after all these matches
You would glove up and defend me too

But when the crowd started cheering
And the bell rang to start the round
I turned back to my corner
And you were nowhere to be found

- Fighting for your love

Niccole Salm

Somebody out there
Faces the dark
Loneliness haunts them
And tears them apart

Hopeless and sleepless nights
Unleash the fear
Wishing and hoping
That someone was there

Here's to the lonely
Love is not what it seems
Sometimes it's a nightmare
It's not always a dream

Love is no fairytale
But we all want it still
Seems like romance never comes your way
But loneliness will

When you turn out the lights
And the days turn to nights
We all desire someone to share our covers
We all just want a lover when you're

Sleeping alone

      -   Here's to the lonely

SHE IS THE SUN

They say
Misery loves company
But I would never wish
This pain upon anyone
No one should feel like this
Even to my enemies
I wish neither harm nor foul
Because sickness in your mind
Always seems to stick around

- Misery loves company

Niccole Salm

I am at war
With my own heart
I fight battles against
My own mind
I crumble in my own hands
Every single time

    -   I am my own worst enemy

I was swallowed up by fear
And a glimpse of hope became
More and more unclear

    -    Pessimistic

If the walls of my bedroom could speak to you

I bet they'd tell my secrets

They'd confess to watching me
Cry myself to sleep
At the end of every day
And sobbing into the night

I bet they'd reveal
How you would never recognize
The girl who has a pillow soaked with tears
The girl who has burning red cheeks
And an aching heart

Trying to figure out
How to hide from the world
That she's falling apart

- These walls

I have a hard time letting go
I hold onto every last bit of hope
With my fingertips
I can't ever find the courage
To unleash my desperate grip

I leave scratches and claw marks
On things that try to leave
Until they slip through my fingers
And finally get away from me

- Holding onto the edge

Niccole Salm

As a kid I thought monsters
Were only hiding under my bed
Turns out the scariest things in the world
Live inside my own head

- Mental illness

SHE IS THE SUN

Nothing that you could say
Would be more hurtful
Than the words I have already spoken
To myself

- Harmful thoughts

I am my own worst enemy
I doubt myself endlessly
But for every single sleepless night
The next day the sun will always shine bright
I'll show the world who I am
And believe in who I become

I fight the fight every day
When I close my eyes and pray
For God knows I am good
Even though at times I'm not so great
And every now and then
The world turns against me once again

Sometimes it makes me angry
But then it makes me stronger
I will always bow my head to pray
When I can't take it any longer

- God help me

SHE IS THE SUN

She hears mom and dad fighting
Through the walls so thin
She thought last time would be the last time
But here they go again

Doors slamming
Walls pounding
Words of hate fill the air
Hostility and anger
She needs a place to hide – but where

Yells and screams can be heard
From every room of the house
Home is supposed to be a safe place
Not meant to be a madhouse

She hides in her room
Bed covers over her head
She can't dream sweet dreams
In a house - where all the love has gone dead

- Broken family

Niccole Salm

I know you think a drink will fix it
Maybe a glass or more
But you know this always turns into
Empty bottles on the floor

Cigarettes in the ash tray
Empty beer cans on the bed
"I can stop anytime I want"
Is what you've always said

I can't change who you are
I can't control what you do
But this is why you've lost your family
How does that feel to you

Does this help you cope
Make you feel better inside
That you chose this life

Then tossed your family aside

- Empty bottles on the floor

Does alcohol make you forget
The things you've said to me

Does alcohol make you forget
All the times you've betrayed me

Does alcohol make you feel
Like you've never done me wrong

Does alcohol make you think
You've been here for me all along

Alcohol may make you forget
All those bad decisions
And all the lies you've ever told
But you're not fooling anyone
The same excuses get pretty old

- Alcoholic tendencies

Niccole Salm

Mentally exhausted
Emotionally drained
Tired of the hate
I need a freaking break

- Exhaustion

SHE IS THE SUN

Responsibilities
Coming at me every which way
Trying to remember
The million things I have to do today

Work never stops
Anxiety piles up
Can't catch a break
Don't know how long it will take…
For life to get better

For my days to get a little bit easier

- Losing hope

Niccole Salm

How many pennies do I have to toss
Backwards into this fountain
Before I can get a sign
Or a damn wish to come true

- All out of coins

SHE IS THE SUN

Dear Mr. Runaway

May I ask what you're running from
Is the weight of the world
Too heavy on your shoulders
So your only option is to run

Can you not bear another moment
Of the mess that we call life
Are you looking for a way out
To find the path that's right

Mr. Runaway
Most people are scared to just walk out
They spend their days unhappy
But they know without a doubt
They all want an escape – and in the world
Just find their place

We all strive for something new
So may I ask…

Can I run away with you?

- Run

Niccole Salm

Stories of Hope…

Niccole Salm

I will never stop writing

For this is my escape
It pulls me through any storm
All the wind and all the rain

It relieves me from my pain
Gives me hope and keeps me sane
Writing gives me a safe space
To say how I feel and be my saving grace

- Thank you, poetry

In the midst of chaos
She became the calm
She always needed

- Clarity

You made me question
My worth
My value
My aspirations
And my dreams
Turns out the problem was

Never even me

- The problem was you all along

You never asked me about my interests
Never asked what I liked to do
Because every time we talked
We only ever talked about you

You never knew that I could write
You probably wouldn't have cared anyway
You never let me take the lead
Or even met me halfway

You really missed out
Better count this as your loss
I'm living life without you
As if our paths never crossed

- Your loss buddy

Niccole Salm

The song that used to make me cry
I now turn on the radio
Sing it at the top of my lungs
Knowing I healed the heartache and
Let all the pain go

- Our song

I don't want to know what you've been doing
Don't need to know where you have been
I just hope you're doing well
And you reflect every now and then

Cause I just want to thank you
For breaking my heart – all those years ago
If it wasn't for the heartache
I would have never had the chance to grow
Into the person I am today
Flaws and all that I am
I love who I became

So thank you once again

- Thank you for breaking my heart

Niccole Salm

I thought losing you
Would be the death of me
Turns out losing you
Brought me back to life

- Born again

The concept of serendipity
Is so profound to me
I can't wrap my head around the fact
That happiness just happens by chance

I've always been told to make a plan
Work towards something
Strive for anything
Find ways to be better
And success doesn't happen by accident

But the serendipitous moments in my life
Happen without premeditated actions
Being at the right place at the right time
Brings us luck
Fortune by coincidence brings us joy

It doesn't need a plan
Didn't have to work towards it
Didn't strive for it
I guess when I wasn't constantly looking
For a better way
The moments of serendipity came

- Happiness by chance

My mind begins to drift
My attention seems to shift

I always find myself daydreaming
Always capture myself thinking
About the future
About the present
About the past

Another moment lost in my thoughts
No wonder why

Life goes by so fast

- Daydreaming

Does the cat who sits on the windowsill

Stare outside in hopes to one day live free
Or rather
Stare at the world around them knowing they rule the home they live in

- Perception

Niccole Salm

First, they say I'm too skinny
And need to gain some weight
Next thing you know they call me fat
And blame me for ending up that way

When I'm blonde
They say brunettes are sexy
When I'm brunette
They say blondes have more fun

Why am I so criticized by everyone?

Opinions of others flow through my brain
Not because I asked for them
But they insist on inflicting pain

Too tall
Too short
Too thick
Too skinny
Man I wish I had a penny
For every time someone
Criticized a woman

    -   I'd be rich

SHE IS THE SUN

Why are you so tall?
They ask me as if I got to create myself in a lab

Why are your arms so long?
They ask me as if my mom went to build-a-kid and
assembled me in a store

I did not get to choose my physical qualities or my
genetic code
It's sad that I have to remind others of what I thought
everyone was mature enough to already know

I have grown to love the body I was given
With all my flaws and imperfections
So don't make me a target
Of all your insecurities and selfish projections

And the next time you ask me
Why I am so tall
I'll let you know that God made me taller so I could
Stand above your hate

And the next time you ask me
Why my arms are so long
I'll tell you it's because God knew my angel wings
Would be longer than yours could ever be

- The way God made me

Niccole Salm

Rest in peace
To the girl who used to care
What everyone thinks

- In loving memory

SHE IS THE SUN

She's a grateful woman and a soldier of love
She'll roll her eyes to hate
And she will always rise above

- Woman warrior

Niccole Salm

Every petal of this rose
Gently falls onto the floor
Every petal holds a wish
Holds a thought
Brings a gift
Another desire added to my list

I'll keep picking
And I'll keep wishing
Until this rose goes bare

For every petal of this rose
Holds purpose as it
Falls through the air

- Rose petals

SHE IS THE SUN

Have you ever laid in the grass
Watching the clouds roll past
Living life in that moment
Feeling grateful for such a wonderful view

- Why can't every moment be this peaceful

Niccole Salm

My biggest fear
Follows me around
Stays on my mind
Consumes my thoughts
And determines my next move

- Scared of settling

Anxiety and panic
Creep up right behind me
Attack my body
Control my mind
Leave me scared and shaky

I feel my heart beating out of my chest
My breath gets short and heavy
As the anxiety takes over me
I feel the knot form inside my belly

My mind tells my body to breathe
To close my eyes and focus
Take a deep breath in
And get my lungs wide open

If I am breathing
I'm still alive

If my heart is beating
I'm still alive

This moment will pass and I will survive

- Talking myself through a panic attack

I'll tend to your battle scars
And try to bring light back into your dark
Healing is a process
It can be slow to start

Don't give up on yourself
Because I'll never give up on you
I know what you're capable of
And I know you know that too

Even though your heart is broken
Beaten black and blue
I promise to hold you steady
And never quit on you

- I'll never give up on you dear

SHE IS THE SUN

May I just say
I think you're really brave
For getting up and getting dressed
Ready to take on another day

I know mornings can be hard
Especially after those nights
When you cried yourself to sleep
Cause with your mind – you fight

Arguing with yourself
Your head telling you – "you're not good enough"
Self-doubt and shame take over
And you feel like giving up

Wishing you had an open wound
That takes a bandage and a patch to seal
Cause the battlefield in your mind
Will take more than first aid to heal

- Depression will not be the death of me

If you thought you knew me a year ago...

You will never recognize me today. I evolved, as did the world around me. I always knew I had several different sides of me like a single piece of a puzzle. I've taken on many roles and have worn many hats of responsibility. I thought I had to hold on to the identity that fit me in that moment of time, forever.

My heart told me it was time to grow, but my mind convinced me that people didn't care. As for all of my other interests - no one ever wanted to know.

So instead - I changed my style, I tried out a nickname, I got some tattoos, I made some risky choices, and I made my personality type fit my new hair color. I thought maybe a superficial change would justify my need for personal growth.

It took me several years of dying my hair to realize I needed change under the surface of my skin rather than the part that everyone sees. The mess that's been locked up and abandoned in my soul was patiently waiting its turn to have my attention. Because when you ignore feelings for so long but the words "I'm fine" come out of your mouth so naturally - you start to believe it too.

If you thought you knew me a year ago...

You would have thought I was fine. Because even that girl that I was would have never recognized the changing, the evolving, and the blooming that came with time.

- Blooming over time

Niccole Salm

You make it sound
Like the process of change
Is a bad thing

- Evolving is sexy

SHE IS THE SUN

Autumn leaves
Fall like me
Onto the ground
As the seasons change
Trying to regrow again

- A new start

Niccole Salm

She will no longer hide
In the darkness of her own shadows
But rather
Turn her silhouette into the star of the show

- Curtain call

SHE IS THE SUN

She's down to earth with a fiery side
She takes risks without the fear of failure
She never takes a sunset for granted
She will bloom
Where she is planted

- Who I want to be

Can I still be an independent woman while wanting
to be in the embrace of a man's arms? Would I still
be considered fearless even though I hesitated before
I jumped?
Could I still be considered strong if I cry when I get
my feelings hurt?
Is it okay to change my mind after I told myself I
would stick it out?

I pull myself in a million different directions.
But yet - I put myself in a box.
Or maybe, everyone else put me in a box,
and I just went along with it?

I want to be a social butterfly, but I like to be in the
comfort of my own home.
I experience emotions on a deeper surface than most.
I want to be able to make quick decisions with no
regret and no guilt.
But - it takes me time to figure out my mood, my
emotions, and how I want to deal with things.

This is why I tend to overthink everything.

I have a strong amount of energy that radiates out of
me, but I try to keep it in, so I don't make a fuss.
Can I still be a feminist even though I don't always
want to argue with a man?
I fight for what I believe in, but sometimes I'm too
tired to fight.

I want to put out fires with love but sometimes I have no more love to give.

I'm in this battle between who I am - and who I want to be.
I am at war between the woman I am - and the woman that people see.

Not too sure who to be – I'm still in the process of discovering me.

- Discovering me

Niccole Salm

Patience is a virtue
Like the calmness in a hurricane
Essential to my life
Like blood flowing through my veins

It pushes me to trust in God
It challenges me to wait my turn
Patience tells me to always back up
Teaches me to wait and learn

To not jump the gun
But rather trust the process
To see what awaits me
Because the best has not come just yet

- Patience child

SHE IS THE SUN

I love coffee in the morning
I love it so much
I get excited about it the night before

I enjoy cute cafes in big cities
I like listening to poetry slams

I could read books for days on end
And when you need a listening ear
I'll always be your friend

    -   Me

Niccole Salm

My mother made me feel
Like I could do anything
Any goals I had
She led me to believe
That I can conquer any quest
And I can pursue any dream
Any bar that I could set
I can earn and achieve

My mother did all she could
To protect me from the world
And now it's up to me
To take it by myself
She said
"One day you'll be on your own"
No one can do it for you

Don't rely on anyone else
If you have dreams and goals
You go and do it for yourself

- My mother's words of wisdom

I'll look the future in the eyes
Because I'm not scared anymore
I'm not scared to fail
I'm not scared of being told no

Because I know you can't get any better
If you never grow

- Courage

Niccole Salm

Her dreams are bigger than average
Her heart filled with courage

Her eyes shine of emerald green
Looking in the face of others saying
"Have a little faith in me"

She didn't need to prove to the world
What she was capable of
But she showed the people anyway
Because she fights all battles with love

- "That" girl

I dance to the beat of my heart
Sing the words on my mind
And let the rhythm of the earth
Define who I am

    -   Free spirit

Niccole Salm

I was born a lover
In a house of fighters
Forced to be tough for no reason
Told to fight back and get even
Forced to be dominant in any situation
Turned me into a nasty combination

Ingrained into my mind
Protect yourself
Protect your heart

I've never wanted to harm
I've never wanted war
I'm just a natural born warrior
With a true heart of gold

Under my armor
I am not a fighter
I'm just a girl
Who craves the real her to shine brighter

- Gold hearted warrior

SHE IS THE SUN

She was created
To hold the sun in her hands
And shine light onto the world
For others to shine
And find their purpose too

- She is the sun

Niccole Salm

Stories of Love…

Niccole Salm

She lit up his life
So bright
Even the sun got jealous

- The jealous sun

SHE IS THE SUN

Drink me up
For I am a cool glass of water
And you've been stranded in the desert heat

- Let me save you

Niccole Salm

I fell in love with an explorer
A man from a foreign land
Someone on a mission
Whose future was not planned

Disembarking from his voyage
He found a forever home
Just like that
He found me as a treasure
Leading him to me like a map

- When an explorer finds his home

SHE IS THE SUN

You came into this country
With no plan and no money
Didn't speak the language of the land
But you took on
Every challenge at-hand

You fought against the odds
You pushed yourself
And prayed to God
That this new life would treat you well
Find happiness
Break you out of your shell

For you left everything you knew behind
Departed your hometown
To pursue a better life

You hunted down what you wanted
Like an archer with his bow and arrow
They paint you as a villain
But you're truly a superhero

- My hero

Niccole Salm

I needed someone
Who could take my broken pieces
And tend to them with care
For they have been shattered too
And had some glue to spare

- Pieced back together

His soul is sweet like honey
And his love is all mine

- Sweet love

Niccole Salm

You fell in love with a wildflower
That dances through the wind
The sun shining down onto me
Telling me to dance again

- Wildflower

SHE IS THE SUN

I'll fight off all your demons
I'll call all of your angels
I'll pull you through the darkest times
I'll always pray for yours and mine

I'll remind you that you're strong
Whenever you feel weak
I'll remind you that you're special
And perfectly unique

I'll take you by the hand
We can face the world together
You'll never be alone
I'll be by your side forever

- Always

Niccole Salm

You make everybody
Feel like someone special

- Your gift

SHE IS THE SUN

I love the way God made you
I wouldn't change a thing
You're truly heaven on earth
The most genuine human being

Your angel wings are purely white
Your heart is truly golden
You're a blessing in disguise
As one who heals the broken

- Healing angel

Roses are red.
Violets are blue.
I fell in love with the boy who –
Left me flowers outside of my house because he was too scared to bring them to my door.
I fell in love with the boy who was so nervous on our Valentine's date - his shaky hands spilled candle wax all over my lap.
I fell in love with the boy who didn't care what *his* friends or *my* family thought of us together, he was going to love me anyway.

We grew together.
We grew apart.
We grew up as different people.
But we did it by each other's side.

Roses are red.
Are violets really blue?
I am still in love with the man who -
Leaves me flowers on *our* kitchen table when he knows I had a hard day.
I am still in love with the man who works 12 hours a day to keep a roof over our head - while I finish my education.
I am still in love with the man who after years of being together - still tells me that I'm beautiful.

I fell even harder for that man -
When he said he would do anything to keep what we have.

Over the years,
the sun didn't always shine.
But even on the rainiest of days -
We cuddled under the umbrella together.

It wasn't always easy.
He broke my heart at times.
But I know I've said things that broke his heart too.
I guess that's what happens in young love.
Roses aren't always red, and violets aren't even blue.

- High school sweetheart

Niccole Salm

You put the air in my lungs
The beat in my heart
You put life back into my tired eyes
You make me feel alive

- Alive

There was a bridge assembled
Over my hellish waters
An overpass was crafted
As the stream got higher and higher
It kept me above the water
So I wouldn't drown in the deepness of the creek

The other side of the river seems like a better view
Then I realized
You built this bridge
So I could get to you

- Dark rivers

Niccole Salm

I am not the creator of the universe
But I can call to existence
A world that's perfect for only me and you

- This is our world, baby

I miss that one-bedroom apartment
With cracks in the ceiling
That let the water in every time it rained
If only I knew then
Those were the best kinds of days

- The good ole days

Niccole Salm

I love the sounds of your voice in the morning
Tired eyes and your hair all a mess
I need a day that's full of rest
A day that's spent with my head laying on your chest

Crawl into bed
Slide next to me
This is how today was meant to be
I could stay right here all day long
Tangled up in you
Is where I know I belong

I'll call up my work
Tell them I can't go
I got a case of love sickness…

And I have to stay home

- Lovesick

SHE IS THE SUN

Your eyes are rich brown like coffee beans
Sitting in my kitchen
Waiting for me to brew and enjoy

Your skin is the color of my coffee
When I add my hazelnut cream
Stirring in the flavor as my mouth starts to salivate

My brain gets excited
And I must confess
This cup of joe will leave me satisfied and delighted

Just like you

- You're my caffeine addiction

Niccole Salm

I bet the top of the world is one hell of a view
But nothing on the planet
Could ever beat looking at you

- What a view

Some days are great
Other days are not

Some days I want to give you the world
Other days I want to take on the world by myself

Some days I want to lay in your arms
And waste the day in bed
Other days we bicker and fight
We go to sleep angry instead

Some days I lead
Other days I follow

Because with you I vowed
To love you through every up
And hold on tight for every down

- Marriage

Niccole Salm

You had all the power in the world
To break my heart
You had every chance to leave
But yet everyday
You kept choosing to love me instead

- Thanks for not leaving

You are my heart and soul
Writing about you is effortless
The poems nearly write themselves

- Effortless poetry

Niccole Salm

Feeling like a princess
At the end of every story
Finally kissed a frog
And found my prince charming

Is this a real-life fairytale
Or am I just being dramatic?
I guess that's what I get
For being a hopeless romantic

- Miss romantic

SHE IS THE SUN

I know you don't want to tell anyone
That you feel alone

Feeling hopelessly unloved
As you fall into your dreams
As your head rests on your pillow
Do you ever think of me?

You're not the only one
Because if you only knew
As I lay myself to sleep
I'm feeling lonely too

- I want you here with me

I envy the way the sun gets to kiss your skin
In the middle of the day

I envy the way the moon catches your attention
In the darkness of the night

I envy the way the wind gets to graze
Across your cheeks on a breezy day

I envy the way the stars get to hear
Your wishes and your dreams
If only your world
Could also include me

- Jealousy

She didn't know
He'd walk into this bar tonight
With his sun-kissed skin
And chocolate eyes

He gives her a look
As if he is thinking
The same as she

She wants to admit to this feeling
She knows he wants to as well
They'll keep this heat between them
A secret they'll never tell

- Bar secrets

Niccole Salm

My ruby red lipstick
Stained your cheek
Your hypnotic eyes
Have possessed me
Ingrained in my mind

Forever

- Ruby red

Gazing into your eyes
Is like looking up at midnight

Seeing millions of sparkling stars
Floating in the milky way
Lighting up the darkness of
Outer space

- Eyes of the galaxy

Niccole Salm

I know what that look means
So you don't have to say a thing
But I hope you can read my mind
Cause I'm way too scared to vocalize
Just how bad I want you

- Mind reader

SHE IS THE SUN

I hope every sunset you watch
Brings you peace at the end of the day
I hope every time you lay in bed
You fold your hands and pray

I hope when you're feeling great
You leave a smile
That's contagious

And I hope when you're feeling blue
You remember who and what
Means the most to you

I hope the world treats you nicely
I hope you find time to take it easy
And even when life feels cruel
I stay hoping that you find
Beauty in the unusual

- My hope

Niccole Salm

Stories
I Treasure the Most…

Niccole Salm

I hope my words
Ignite a flame
And those strong enough
Who can take the heat
Let these words burn into their minds

- Listen

You thought I was like the tides
Crashing into the shore
Nothing but a shallow water wave
But honey
I'm the whole damn hurricane

- Miss tropical storm

Niccole Salm

If you thought revenge
Left a salty after-taste
I must warn you of all the hell
A girl like me can raise

- You should be worried

SHE IS THE SUN

Poured fuel on my fire
Woke the beast inside me
Set me off like a wildfire
Burning acres across the country

- Uncontrollable flame

Niccole Salm

What do you see when you look at me
Do you see someone who has overcome challenges?
Do you see someone who had to develop resilience?
Do you see someone who has had to face their fears?

No matter what you see
When you look at me
I've taken the time
To take a look on the inside
I've worked so hard for my goals
I've come too far to give in now

I've pushed myself
And did what I had to do
I could never quit
Even if I wanted to

- Resilience

I'm breaking out of the chains
I wrapped around
Myself

- Unleashed

Niccole Salm

I used to be different
Had a mindset of weakness
Until one day I realized
You must run faster than the lion
Before you become his dinner

- You are predator or you are prey

The mountains stand alone in the night
But instead of weeping to the moon
I decided to run with the wolves

- Wolfpack

She carries herself like a woman
She leads the pack like a boss
She does whatever - whenever the hell she wants

She acts like a lady
She's no damsel in distress
Honey
Her queendom is the one
Who rules all the rest

- Thy queendom come

SHE IS THE SUN

They call me mean
Because I don't let others
Push me around
And mess with me

Or do they call me names
To save face
Because they don't want a female
To put them in their place

- Stop calling women bitches

Don't tell me what I can and cannot do

Don't try
To put me in my place
Tell me how to act
Or tell me what I should and should not say

Because if you haven't noticed
My wings spread farther
Than your insecurities

And your beliefs
Of what a woman should do and think
Will not be the rules I live by

- Feminism

You tried calling checkmate
As if your foolish moves
Were ever threatening to me

- I already won the game

Niccole Salm

I'm sorry
If you thought my kindness
Was disguised as flirtation

Maybe next time
You should assume that women
Are not kind -
Because we desire you

But rather we are kind
Because we desire others to be kind too

- No, I wasn't flirting

SHE IS THE SUN

She's a single mother
Who keeps pushing for a better life
She's wishing
To give her kids a fighting chance

She spends her whole life working
Providing for her children
She always puts her loved ones before herself

Her love outpours naturally
She loves her kids 'til infinity
She never thinks twice
About her choices and her sacrifice

Cause she's got the heart of a woman

- This one is for you, mom

Niccole Salm

Maybe it's the way
She carries herself
Or maybe it's the way
She cares for everyone else
That makes her overflow with grace

- Graciousness

I don't need you
To slay my dragons
I don't need you
To fight my demons

I'd rather protect myself instead
For I know there are always better days ahead

- Hopeful

I can be quite stubborn
But I fight passionately for what I believe in
I always stand up for the people I love
And I'll have the backs of those close to me

My loyalty is a strength of mine
It's something I am most proud of
I do my best to do no harm
But I always stand my ground
And defend myself when needed

I am calm but I am ambitious
I guess that's the Taurus in me
Oh and did I not mention?
I'm kind of a sucker for astrology

- Earth signs

Golden skies
Bring peace to my mind
Grace in my heart
And hope for the future

- Stay golden

Niccole Salm

I desire to be a child again
Wishing upon stars
Picking flower petals
Dreams so wild yet so gentle

I desire to have the youthful spirit
I had when I was young
The whole world was in my hands
Taking on the future with no plan

I desire to have the eyes of a child
Full of hope by all means
Spending my young days chasing crazy dreams

- To be a child once again

SHE IS THE SUN

Let the rain cleanse the earth
Let the sun heal my soul
Let the caged bird sing
Let the universe take control

A child of the stars
Dancing gracefully around the moon
Pink skies shining calmly
Provide beauty in the late afternoon

Let every day rejuvenate
And bring your heart much peace
Be an admirer of the world
For this creation is a masterpiece

- Masterpiece

Niccole Salm

Took me years to realize
That if the world is calling out to you…

Listen

- When the universe speaks

I crave to go with the flow
Just want to breathe in and let go

Why do I need a plan
Why do I need a straight path
I don't want my life set in stone like that

I don't need a road
More or less traveled
I don't need to wish upon a star
I don't want to know if my last days
Are waiting near or far

As for the future
I'd rather just not know
Because I choose to follow the path
In whichever way the wind will blow

- Direction of the wind

Poems are words from the soul
Feelings straight from the heart

Words
Catchy like a song
But not quite as loud

Stories
Flow like motion pictures
Like films with no sound

Poems tell the words that can't be spoken
But can't be kept inside
Words that must be set free
In order to survive

Poems are a gift
One that keeps giving
The more I live
The more I feel
The more I hurt
The more I experience every moment of the day
The more words of a poem I have to say

- The words of a poem

Thank You...

Niccole Salm

Well, you made it to the end of my book. You read page by page the words of my soul. I can't thank you enough for giving my poetry a chance to enter your own heart. If you take anything from this book - I hope you understand that even when you feel hopeless because life can be unfair, WE have the power to determine what we become. WE have the power to become our most unstoppable selves.

- Thank you, thank you, thank you from the bottom of my heart

Again, I really appreciate you taking the time to read my book. If you want to contact me, you can reach me at niccolesalmpoetry@gmail.com or find me on Instagram @niccolesalm

"With poetry, you don't have to say a lot in order to have a lot to think about"

- Grandpa Salm

Niccole Salm

Until Next Time…

Made in the USA
Monee, IL
20 February 2022